The Present Colonizes the Past

The Future Forsaken?

ROMILA THAPAR

Seagull Books

LONDON NEW YORK CALCUTTA

POINTS OF VIEW / I

Professor Romila Thapar delivered the
Third Dr Kapila Vatsyayan Memorial Lecture,
organized by the Kapila Vatsyayan Memorial Committee,
at the India International Centre, New Delhi,
on 16 September 2025.

This edition is an expanded version of the lecture.
The original may be heard on YouTube.

Seagull Books, 2026

First published by Seagull Books, 2026

ISBN 978 1 80309 661 2

British Library Cataloguing-in-Publication Data
A catalogue record for this book
is available from the British Library

Typeset by Seagull Books, Calcutta, India

How does the present reshape what a society chooses to remember as its past?

Recent interpretations of India's history have replaced careful inquiry with narratives that mirror contemporary anxieties and ambitions, sidelining the evidence, debate and plurality that once characterized India's long intellectual tradition. At stake is a shift from understanding history as a method to treating it as a tool of identity and authority.

In *The Present Colonizes the Past*, Romila Thapar asks: How have cultural and religious identities evolved through interaction rather than isolation? How have dissent and accommodation shaped social change? How have education and public discourse influenced what is accepted as knowledge? And, most urgently, how might weakened institutions and selective pasts redefine our heritage and citizenship?

ROMILA THAPAR is Emeritus Professor of History at the Jawaharlal Nehru University, New Delhi. A former General President of the Indian History Congress, she is a Fellow of the British Academy and an Honorary Fellow of Lady Margaret Hall, Oxford, and SOAS, London. In 2008 she received the Library of Congress's Kluge Prize.

POINTS OF VIEW

The Present Colonizes the Past

I WAS INVITED to deliver the Kapila Vatsyayan Memorial Lecture 2025, and it was suggested to me that I should speak on history: on the rather contentious relationship that has now developed between professional history writing and that which goes by the name of history across various media, often written, it seems, by people unfamiliar with the historical method and some even with the subject itself. Barring a few exceptions, much of what they say interprets the past as they wish, even when it lacks proven evidence.

This type of distortion of the historical past has obvious implications for the interpretation of history, but its influence is not confined to interpretation alone. There are at least three other areas in which it has a determining role. These are: the concepts we use to define our cultural heritage; the propagation of inaccurate history, which is contributing to the lowering of our educational standards; and the use of history to legitimize a particular political ideology.

I believe that we need a much fuller and sharper understanding of the problematic impact that prejudiced versions of history, driven by polemicists, have on our society's thinking. Further, we need to ask why those in authority often discourage the thoughtful exploration of historical knowledge.

Being a historian is a discipline. I will say more later about the nature of historiography, or the methodology of reaching a sound historical understanding. For now, I want to underline that even the best of historians—

perhaps *especially* the best of historians—must always be aware of their own possible biases and influences in interpreting the past. However, when narratives of the past are driven by biases, they can become fantasy.

The attitude of those who write, or claim to write, history varies. Professional and academic historians, and others who train themselves to write carefully considered history, insist on using evidence of proven reliability. The larger number of others who use the media as their platform are often least concerned with evidence and make statements without checking their veracity.

Let me, however, clarify that I am not critiquing everyone who writes on historical subjects but is not a professional historian. Some writers, despite not being professional historians, contribute valuable work in historical research. They can be identified by the evidence they use as sources and their reliance on logical and rational arguments in their analyses. They generally seek serious and well-informed discussion of their work, often engaging with professional historians and publishing in select journals.

Rather, my criticism is of those who write on historical subjects but base their writing on negligible research. They approach historical events with a populist agenda and often project their writing through mainstream and social media. Currently, it is their views of the past that predominate in state-sponsored educational programmes.

Professional history in India over the past half-century has undergone an immense change in the range of sources, in methods of analysing those sources, and in explanations of what happened in the past. Historical research now goes far beyond dynastic history, and incorporates aspects of social, economic, cultural and environmental history. This increase in curiosity about the past and the world we live in is commendable. History is no longer just an aspect of Indology—that is, providing information on the past. It is now an analytical discipline explaining the complexities of the past. These concern not only the 'what' and the 'where' of past events, but also the 'how' and the 'why' of what happened. Asking new questions has led to the emergence of new methods of obtaining data and investigating it. This involves fresh interpretations that often question older knowledge. When existing interpretations become invalid, they are discarded, as, for example, some long-held colonial readings of the Indian past.

These changes in historical research are exciting intellectual developments, making historical understanding a dynamic field. Nevertheless, it still relies on proven evidence, not guesses and fantasies.

HISTORY HELPS US CLARIFY what we call our cultural identity. This is central to the perception of who we are and what we are about, which in turn is pivotal to our understanding of ourselves and our cultures—our patterns of living. Historical sources from the past provide many narratives of persons and events from early times, in a variety of texts. Initially, the past was remembered as part of an oral tradition of what was believed to have happened. Some versions were then recorded in texts such as the epics—the

Mahabharata and the *Ramayana*—regarded more as literary compositions and religious literature than as historical writing. Some of these were consulted by historians, hoping to find nuggets of history embedded in them.

Categories of texts in Sanskrit and Prakrit that align more closely with what we today call history began to appear from the later first millennium CE and included, for example, the charitas (biographies), such as Banabhatta's *Harshacharita*, the historical biography of the king Harshavardana of Kannauj; and the vamshavalis (chronicles) of regions and dynasties, the best-known being Kalhana's *Rajatarangini*, the history of Kashmir. Continuing the practice in the second millennium CE were the tarikhs (chronicles), written in Persian, such as the *Tarikh-i-Firoz Shahi*, the chronicle of the reign of the Sultan Firuz Shah Tughlaq. In modern times, providing the evidence for any statement based on a text has become a crucial factor in reconstructions of the past that are defined as history. Early societies, however, paid less attention not only to providing evidence but also to proving its authenticity. Working with textual evidence demanded that the historian have a further basic qualification: knowledge of the languages in which the text was written.

However, when it came to explaining the past—that is, explaining why and how an event occurred, rather than just recording what happened—the deeper imprint in modern writing came initially from the colonial reading and reconstruction of the Indian past. European readings of Asian history accompanied the establishment of colonialism. These readings were obsessed with a single explanation of Asian history, and this was what they called Oriental Despotism. Colonial writers maintained that the earlier rulers of Asia were despots governing impoverished peasants through an oppressive bureaucracy. The bureaucracy collected taxes in both money and in kind. Some writers maintained that the despots also had full control over the hydraulic system of irrigation, bringing in large agricultural yields that constituted the wealth of the despot. These were therefore called 'hydraulic societies'. It was also argued that there was no notion of a state, all authority being in the hands of the despot. Since such rulers did not have to claim legitimacy from the past, recourse to history was not a feature of their societies. Arguing that there was an absence of historical writing from the pre-colonial past, colonial authorities wrote their version of the history of the colony. This was effectively in accordance with what they believed it to be—that is, they invented it in line with their own preconceived views as well as the requirements of the present that they wished to legitimize by claiming they had been inherited from past times.

As a result, the writing of Indian history in modern times began with colonial theories about the Indian past. The one theory that was applied to all Asian history was Oriental Despotism. Apart from this, two theories in particular were deeply ingrained and initially shaped Indian history. These were the Aryan theory of race and the two-nation theory.

The Aryan theory of race assumes that Indian history began when the subcontinent was settled by the Aryans, a superior race of migrants from Central Asia. Upper-caste Hindus claim descent and cultural origins from the Aryans, and Hinduism claims its roots in their religious ideas and practices.

The two-nation theory was initially set out by James Mill in the early nineteenth century. It stated that India consisted of two nations—the Hindu and the Muslim—and that they were permanently hostile to each other. The aggression was said to be essentially motivated by Muslim invaders constantly attacking the settled Hindu society. The communal interpretation that evolved from this theory held that the religious aggression between Hindus and Muslims explained the history of the second millennium CE. It was, and still is, argued by those who are generally not historians that, since the Muslims were in positions of authority, the aggression took the form of Muslims victimizing Hindus.

These interpretations of Indian history were questioned half a century ago by professional historians and a few others and have since been discarded. Both Sanskrit and Persian texts and inscriptions point to a relationship between the host cultures and new arrivals in the subcontinent that was occasionally conflictual but, far more often, took the form of an accommodating interface that became acceptable to both. Invasions there were, motivated by territorial aggrandizement accompanied by political control, and these were not unconnected with the ambitions of earlier times, when there was no lack of violent confrontations between kingdoms. However, with Yavanas from West Asia and Turushkas from Central Asia, as the Arabs and Turks were called in Sanskrit sources, there was also a mixing of cultures and the emergence of new sects and social groups, with evolving degrees of integration, not to mention changes in social and economic patterns coming about through increasing interaction, as, for instance, in activities linked to commerce.

However, at the popular level today, the unhistorical versions of what happened in medieval times have been kept alive, propagated in Hindutva and similar ideologies and among those who popularize such views.

Among professional historians, the Aryan theory of race and the two-nation theory were replaced by other explanations based explicitly on evidence that was verified and analysed. There was a move away from colonial views that focused mainly on dynastic and political history, and historical research now included other aspects of social, economic and political functioning. Two substantial and extensive changes were introduced into historical research: the adoption of a historical method as a procedure for research, and, where possible, the comparative use of interdisciplinary studies. These provided alternative explanations for what happened, and why.

LET ME EXPLAIN what is meant by the historical method. It is the orderly investigation, step by step, of a historical problem. The first step, after deciding the theme to be researched, is the collection of data from a range of sources, some of which may not have been consulted previously or examined from diverse perspectives. The data must come from verified evidence. It cannot be hearsay, or come from posts on social media or WhatsApp, or be the wishful thinking of the writer. Furthermore, the information from sources—texts and artefacts—should not be merely quoted and repeated but analysed afresh from various perspectives. This is particularly important where sources are in more than one language, such as Persian, Sanskrit and the regional languages for medieval history.

This is important because, for example, what is now labelled as the period of medieval history (circa 1200 to 1750 CE), was earlier called the Muslim period, based on the two-nation theory of James Mill, and much of it therefore relied largely on Persian sources. Now, however, texts in Sanskrit and the regional languages are being consulted more extensively, yielding differences in historical thinking about those times and frequently contradicting the colonial and subsequent communal interpretations.

Seeking explanations about the past requires an intensive study of the sources. Who was the author of the material? Did his background influence what he wrote? Did he have an agenda? Was the agenda successfully conveyed by the text? Did it propagate a belief or a point of view projected as infallible, and was it questioned? How was the text received? For what audience was it written—the royal court, a community of monks, or the larger public? As I'm sure is clear from this, asking the right questions and finding the answers are both complex and require thoughtful reading and knowledge of the sources.

After assembling the evidence, causal and explanatory connections between people and events can be investigated. These connections must draw on logical and rational arguments, not on guesses or probabilities dictated by the writer's preferences.

The introduction of interdisciplinary research resulted in historians becoming aware of methods of analysis used in other disciplines that might also be useful to their research. It added more data to the historical evidence, as well as prompting fresh questions. An example of this was what became the more extensive meaning of the word 'culture'. From referring only to the thinking, writing and activities of elite groups, it came to mean the pattern of living of any group. Hence the significance of introducing the idea that a society in its entirety may host many cultures—that is, patterns of living specific to different groups. Large, complex societies incorporating diverse cultural patterns had to be studied to explain why such diversity existed, the nature of the interface among different groups, and the connecting links where they existed.

For early history, in addition to archaeology, comparative analyses from linguistics and from social and economic anthropology are occasionally suggestive, such as in defining cultures. Currently there is also evidence from environmental studies and from genetics. All this makes the analysis of the evidence richer and more insightful. For instance, religions are no longer viewed in isolation but are seen as closely related to the kinds of societies in which they flourished. This helps explain the forms that some beliefs have taken and the kinds of patrons they had in their propagation.

Let me give you another example of changes from earlier research. In the eighteenth and nineteenth centuries, William Jones and Max Müller studied the Vedic texts, and the main study was related to language and philology—namely, investigating the structure, development and relationships of languages. These texts and their studies became the bedrock of understanding Indian society, belief and thought. Indo-Aryan was studied in isolation, despite being recognized as a cognate of Iranian Aryan and having elements of non-Aryan languages. The discovery of the Indus civilization, with its as-yet unread script and language, and its possibly non-Aryan character, added another dimension to the study of language.

Later studies of linguistic aspects of Vedic texts suggested the presence of some non-

Indo-Aryan elements. This raised the question of whether there had been a cultural interaction, however limited, between Aryan and non-Aryan speakers and, in turn, whether this had had any impact on the evolving Aryan culture. These non-Aryan elements are found only in Vedic Sanskrit. They do not occur in other cognate languages, such as Iranian-Aryan or early Celtic. So, the cultural interaction that we might infer was limited to the areas in which the Vedic texts were first composed—the Panjab and the north-west of the subcontinent. References to the dasas in the *Rigveda*, for example, have now begun to receive more attention, not just in themselves but also in the way they may reflect their interaction, however marginal, with Aryan culture.

Genetic identities based on DNA samples from skeletal remains in this geographical area can be problematic when discussed in relation to the broader picture of identities and origins, with the hint of a migrant connection.

Migrations into India from various directions were very frequent in history, and Indians migrating to other places, often following trade, was also not uncommon. This illustrates how research of almost every kind contains an initial element of speculation until incontrovertible evidence is established, which is why proven evidence is crucial.

Coming back to the research of Jones and Müller, the identity of the Indo-Aryan speakers was the initial question—namely, whether they were indigenous to the subcontinent, as is one popular belief, or were migrants from further north, who gradually had a cultural interface with the local cultures in India, as academic historians now believe.

A QUESTION MUCH DEBATED in the controversies over history today is that of the origin and evolution of Hinduism and of the Hindus. In the absence of a single founder, teacher or prophet, as in the Abrahamic religions, the idea of multiple points of origin seems to present problems for some commentators. Evidence relating to these origins does not support a single, uniform identity, unchanging and static for all time. What is of interest to historians studying various societies is how cultural identities evolve—what aspects of culture were drawn from whom, and what was transmitted and to whom. We know that wherever there have been migrations, populations have not just become mixed but, from the mixing of cultures and patterns of living, fresh cultural forms have often emerged. The many well-established migrations of people coming from Central Asia over the last two millennia and settling in North India—the Shakas, Kushans, Hunas, Turushkas—and those who came from West Asia—Yavanas / Arabs, who settled along the west coast of India—were not silent spectators of a static culture. A new culture emerged each time, as is reflected in the objects, identities and thoughts we have inherited from them.

Many groups have mingled and defied segregation. This makes it problematic to establish identities that claim to have originated in past times and from a single source. Race itself is a dated and debated concept, as is purity of race, and it is now largely set aside in population studies. But it was used in the nineteenth century under the aegis of colonialism and was emphasized as one of the features that separated the colonizer from the colonized. The categories were often uncertain, some determined by skin colour and physical features.

The discovery and extensive excavation of sites of the Indus civilization in the twentieth century gave visibility to prior non-Aryan cultures. More recent excavations in the peninsula have brought to light what appear to have been cultures contemporary with the late and post-Harappan. The history of this period is more complicated than it was thought to be until recently. These new sources of history and the explanations that they bring have altered the narrative of the history of the second and first millennia BCE and occasioned extensive debate among professional historians.

The evolution of Indian society continued with changes, large or small, emerging from the social groups, both indigenous and alien, each group identified initially by its culture—that is, its pattern of living and the ideas and objects it identified with. This was not necessarily a social upheaval but involved the acculturation of communities settled in the subcontinent, and the process continued through history until the establishment of colonialism. Cultures mingled at many levels. Some resulted from the juxtaposition of elite groups, others from the interaction among those at other social levels whose occupations often brought them together, as in the case of various craftsmen. New cultures emerged and most found a niche for their particular idiom. Indian society has not been singular and uniform. It was a society of plural articulations, like many other pre-modern societies, evolving from diverse cultural forms.

Adjustments to cultural change among these various constituents brought agreement and disagreement, acceptance by some and resistance by others. There were differences of thought, opinion and actions. The mid-first millennium BCE to the mid-first millennium CE was a period of lively interchange accompanied by both dissent and consent. This is characteristic of acculturation. Brahmanas referred to the Shramanas—that is, the Buddhists, Jainas and Ajivikas—as nastikas, or non-believers, therefore belonging to a separate category in religious and social mapping, and at times placed low in the social hierarchy. But since there was no majoritarianism in those days, groups and leaders needed to assert their dominance in other ways, such as by claiming proximity to power or insisting on high ranking in social hierarchies.

Edicts of the Mauryan emperor Ashoka plead for tolerance among the *Bahmanam-Samanam* (Brahmanas and Shramanas), as he refers to them. Patanjali was not joking when he compared the relationship between Brahmanas and Shramanas to that between the snake and the mongoose. Debate and dissent were familiar to Indian intellectuals of past times and were recorded and discussed. Those in authority, in some instances, did try to silence them, but did not succeed. Dissent continued to have a strong presence.

The practice of openness did, therefore, prevail, and more so in sections of society that did not need to be conservative or orthodox. Despite what James Mill and Friedrich Max Müller maintained, there was an interface among communities, with cultural borrowings that pertained to both religious and social practices. This led to the evolving of a large number of sects among various sections of society.

Then, in the late second millennium CE, came the collision of colonial conquest. India's colonial era was the first time that there was no acculturation with a dominant power. The law of sedition, the banning of books, the arrest of those who were critical of authority, are known from the colonial encounter—and have unfortunately continued. Unlike other previous rulers who came from outside India, conquered and settled here, the colonial rulers conquered but did not settle. Even where they did settle, as in North America, Australia or parts of Africa, the earlier local populations were in many places either annihilated or victimized. In India, however, they remained permanent aliens.

One could ask whether this pattern of colonialism can perhaps be attributed to a Protestant ethic as well as to particular kinds of economic requirements, since the pattern of colonialism endorsed by Iberian Catholics gave rise to a different pattern of mestizo populations and cultures. The wealth of India was appropriated and directed to distant Britain, the homeland of the colonial power. This had a positive impact on the economic rise of Britain. Control over India was exercised by controlling the economy, by putting the people to work to make the colony productive for the new conquerors, and also, less directly, by imprinting their own comprehension of India on the Indian middle class.

In the period after independence, this imprint began to be questioned and debated by educated Indians. But what is being propagated as Indian history today in educational institutions and in much of the media is a return to the discarded colonial theories. These have been resurrected in Hindutva history. This is not the decolonization that it claims to be, since, ironically, it is based on the colonial theories.

LET ME BRIEFLY SUMMARIZE the Hindutva theory of Indian history, which is now being taught and propagated. It essentially returns to the colonial theories of the superiority of the Aryan race and the two-nation theory. The Aryan race, according to this view, is said to be indigenous to India, superior to all, and ancestral to the Hindus and Hinduism. It maintains that India was the territory within which were located the *pitribhumi*, or ancestral land of the Hindus, and the *punyabhumi*, or the land that gave rise to the religion of the

Aryans, the foundation of Hinduism. The dominant status of the Hindus, therefore, cannot be questioned, as it is claimed to go back to the very origins of India. This, in turn, allows them to claim superiority over other groups and religions. Such an identity becomes a major asset today for justifying Hindu majoritarianism in addition to its numerical strength. Both claims are necessary to the Hindu identity as envisaged by Hindutva. This is the pivot of its ideology, which is legitimized through its version of the past. In this 'history', the political requirements of the present colonize the past and incorporate colonial theories. How, then, will this define our future?

evolve from the interface of cultures, when historical changes affect existing forms of belief. Speaking very broadly, the origins and the continuity of Hinduism display an impressive diversity that has given to Hinduism the very special character that distinguishes it from other major religions. Its historical evolution had a different emphasis from those of the Abrahamic religions.

Since religion, and especially Hinduism, has become so central to politics and the general ambience in India, I would like to take a quick look at my thoughts on the subject from a historical perspective. The roots of religion in India are traced back to the Harappan religion of the north-west and, in the peninsula, to the megalithic and other cultures. The differences between early and later periods are striking. In the late second and first millennia BCE, Vedic belief required worship at large open-air altars for sacrificial rituals. In later times, from the late first millennium CE onwards, as different rituals were introduced, these altars were mentioned less frequently and their associated rituals come to be linked more closely with royalty. In earlier times, the prominent deities were Mitra and Varuna, as well as Indra and Agni. The Vedic deities and rituals continued, but the Puranic texts of the first millennium CE gave greater prominence to other deities and other forms of worship, such as Durga as well as other goddesses. The focus now shifted to Shiva and Vishnu, and to new ways of representing and worshipping them.

Of these, the more prestigious involved the worship of icons placed inside temples scattered across the subcontinent and built by those who could afford to do so. This was an innovation, since earlier icons and halls of worship had been associated mainly with the Shramana religions, especially Buddhism. Other religions of lesser social status also had icons, but of a different kind and worshipped in various ways. The Vedic phase continued, though less prominently, and Puranic Hinduism in its various new forms gradually became the dominant religious presence.

Then came the subcontinental efflorescence in the multiple expressions of Bhakti and their interface with variant regional cultures, from the late first millennium CE in the peninsula and in the second millennium across northern India. The regional formulations were not the same. There was some uniformity at elite levels, but local deities and rituals provided the larger religion with distinctive differences. These included diversity in the worship of major deities, and both teaching and worship increasingly incorporated regional languages. We can only imagine what the reaction would have been had some of the bhakts and sants from different places actually met and conversed. The worship of Jagannath in Odisha and of Vitthala / Vithoba in Maharashtra differed in terms of the mythology, representation, rituals and texts of worship, although the deity was the same.

Differences are significant, as they often result from inducting local beliefs and forms related to religious ideas that come from different strata of society and may have different origins. Nevertheless, these diverse forms lived in juxtaposition in the various regions of the subcontinent, and inter-relations ranged from cordiality and borrowing to distancing. Religious sects were conceding the centrality of the audience in their thinking.

The second millennium CE was also the time when an array of Sufi teachers migrated from Central Asia, some with Persian connections, to India. They established themselves at various locations across the subcontinent. They soon established their own institutions, in particular the khanqahs, which became centres where Sufis gathered and, gradually, where some non-Sufi supporters also assembled. The message of love for the deity in the abstract or the teacher and the concept of renunciation as significant to belief drew together people of differing ideologies. This inevitably led to a considerable interface with the local culture, giving rise to many fresh sects carrying religious messages, some new in thought and some reformulating earlier ideas.

Initially, there was a substantial input from Islam, but gradually the dialogue with the various established sects led to new sectarian variations that reflected elements of the prevailing formal religions as well as other belief systems. Dialogues such as those between the Nathpanthis and Sufi sects in the Panjab have been written about, and similar exchanges also occurred in the peninsula. Guru Nanak, for instance, is said to have had many conversations with teachers of these varied belief systems.

Religious movements and teachings of consequence are rarely pristine and entirely innovatory. They tend to carry, in varying degrees, elements of existing beliefs and practices. This was evident in the evolution of the various Sufi sects which, given their Iranian and Central Asian provenance, retained elements of earlier prevalent religions of the area such as the Zoroastrian, Manichaean and Buddhist. The messages of love and compassion in human behaviour, and the importance of renunciation—features of these earlier religions—were not lost on them. Such teachings were part of the introductory dialogue with local sects when they settled in India, and this was facilitated by the openness of the teaching and practices of many Bhakti sects. What we have to remember is that the Sufis who came to India did not just represent another wave of conventional Islam. They belonged to religious sects that had already adjusted to some of the non-Islamic religions from which they came—one of which, Buddhism, had itself originated in India.

The seventeenth-century poet Abdul Rahim Khan-i-Khanan, a high-ranking dignitary in Akbar's court, was a scholar of much achievement in Persian; he also composed couplets in praise of Krishna in one of the Bhakti traditions of worship. The dialogues of such people effectively crossed religious boundaries. Depending on regional factors, elements of other belief systems either seeped in or else were disregarded or negated. A fascinating example of this is the word used for God in the Panjabi language and in Sikhism, which is *Rabb*—originally the Arabic word for the same. It speaks of a remarkable cultural ambience. These phases of the predominant religion in India did not fade away. They have survived the centuries, sometimes in strength, sometimes diluted, and sometimes in remnants. They are observed to varying degrees and forms by a variety of Hindus today, although they are also dismissed by some.

In exploring sectarian relationships, I am not suggesting that they were all harmonious and without conflict. This cannot be assumed, because we know that contentions when perceived as irreconcilable can lead to conflict. However, such conflicts are not invariably over religious differences; in fact, they more often arise over differences of a social nature—politics, caste conflict or economic disparity—and should not, therefore, be invariably labelled as a religious conflict. There is a tendency to describe all conflicts in medieval times as stemming from religious differences between Hindus and Muslims, an imprint of the two-nation theory. Yet, on analysis, most of these conflicts are seen to have quite other causes. The same argument would apply to the pre-Islamic period, when there were just as many conflicts: a few of which were indeed linked to religious differences, but most arose from a broader range of incompatibles.

Colonial times brought another turn in Hindu thought and belief, evident in the emergence of what came to be called the Samajs. Among the upper echelons of Hindu society, some of these were thought of as reform movements intended to simplify Hindu belief and ritual in conformity with what was thought to be a more modern way of projecting religion—for example, in matters relating to the practices required of women. In some instances, the formulation was in keeping with the middle-class projection of itself; otherwise, it was a fresh way of formulating the religion. The Sanatan Dharma, which claims to be a belief system that has existed since eternity, was given much publicity in the nineteenth century in the attempt to state that Hinduism was a singular and uniform religion for all time and space.

One of the challenges of studying religions in India is that sects, the usual unit of focus, have historically often extended in varying ways across more than one belief system. And it is also possible that uniformity and adherence to rules may have prevailed among a smaller proportion of believers as compared to present times. We often forget that the dominant religion in India did not require a formal conversion. Social regulations seem to have been of greater consequence. One could choose one's deity (if required) and one's way of expressing devotion and reverence. This aspect is, unfortunately, not being sufficiently explored by those interpreting the Hindu religion as a belief system. It had a historical evolution as well as a religious personality. The ways in which it is articulated in practice are, not unexpectedly, unlike the forms familiar to Europe and beyond.

GOING BACK TO COLONIAL TROPES about Indian history, however, once the two-nation theory was accepted it was not too difficult to make the Hindu the primary citizen, with non-Hindus having a secondary status. In the Hindutva version of history, based on the colonial reading, the supposed two nations—the Hindu, established four thousand years ago, and the Muslim, established one thousand years ago—were projected as having always been in conflict, with the latter denying the superior position of the former in Indian society. According to the Hindutva view, the culture of India has always been predominantly Hindu, although it is said to have been in conflict with the nastikas, to begin with—a conflict that would seem to have been resolved in favour of the Hindus—but then for the last thousand years the Hindus have suffered by being victimized by the Muslims. This view continues to maintain that the rightful future of India lies in its reverting to being a Hindu state, the Hindu Rashtra. The inheritance of Hindu superiority has now to be asserted.

Professional historians have contradicted the theory that the Hindus and Muslims were distinctively altogether different and had a relationship that was permanently hostile. And, logically, this could hardly hold for a society where, in most spheres of life and occupations, there was a close interdependence of the two. In occupations where the technology of early times required the co-operation of different levels of expertise in the production of goods, it would have been normal for persons of both communities to work together. This is what the sources, when consulted across languages, suggest.

The builders of monuments were often local, as their records in Sanskrit inscriptions on the monuments show, and they worked at times with architects from elsewhere. The weavers were often local Muslims, as at Chanderi, but the traders who sold their textiles were frequently local Hindu textile merchants—and the two had to work in unison. The soldiers were largely local recruits, along with some mercenaries, who served in the armies of any ruler who employed them, irrespective of who was at war with whom. Those who painted the superb miniature paintings at the various courts of both Hindu and Muslim rulers came from both communities. Among scholars, poets and writers there was much fraternizing in the pursuit of literary and philosophical interests. At elite levels, Hindu princesses were married to Muslim noblemen. Owing to such intermarriages with preceding Mughal emperors, Shah Jahan was three-quarters Rajput in origin and only one-quarter Mughal.

This is not to suggest that there were no hostilities between the Mughals and the local rulers. The Mughals wished to acquire territory to create a kingdom, so they laid siege to and attacked the forts of local Rajputs and other rulers and fought battles with them. The latter resisted as much as they could, but, as frequently happens in such conquests, there was peace making after the conflict. These were political wars, often to protect or regain kingdoms, and not religious wars. They were battles between two political powers and not between two religions. The Mughals had Hindu Rajput generals commanding their armies, and the Rajputs had the descendants of the Afghan ruler Sher Shah Suri and their contingents as allies. The Mughals fought and defeated the Suris as well, which allowed them to consolidate their power in the middle

Ganges plain. What gave the Mughals a base in India was that, after defeating Ibrahim Lodi at Panipat, Babur acquired the territories of the Lodi Sultanate. One Muslim was fighting another. This was not a religious war but a political one.

There were some conflicts, as indeed there had been among groups even in earlier times, but these cannot be described as the victimization of Hindus. Where there were cases of victimization, we may recall that this behaviour was not unknown to Indian society: for many centuries there had been the victimization of the avarna—those without caste—by the savarna—those of caste. Such victimization continued into later times. That this persisted even among those converted to Islam—where, in theory, all men are equal—is evident from the existence of the excluded castes of Pasmanda Muslims, probably the avarnas of earlier times who were unable to expunge their caste identity. Wealthy upper-caste Hindus on one occasion at least even referred to the Muslim sultan as a mleccha in an inscription, presumably because he did not have a caste identity, or, not being a caste Hindu, was regarded as of low status.

The supposed racial and cultural superiority of the supposedly indigenous Aryans, and the supposedly permanent conflict between Hindus and Muslims, are now propagated through the media. Such statements find no place in academic journals, and they certainly cannot be taken as historically accurate. But when this becomes the basis of educational curricula and comes to displace history, it is a serious matter. It obstructs knowledge systems. Even if erroneous, it is nevertheless imprinted in social attitudes. It also raises questions about a wider dimension of our culture—namely, that of Indian pluralism.

Historically, and up to the present, multiple sects constitute what is called Hinduism. Its pluralism makes its history recognizably different from that of the

Abrahamic religions. What will current narratives do to the inherent pluralism of Hinduism, with its accommodation of diverse co-existing sects that, for its believers, endows it with a unique richness?

There are also consequences for how we conceptualize nationalism. During colonial times, nationalism was often qualified and understood as anti-colonial nationalism. Anti-colonial nationalism endorsed the essentials of democracy and secularism, even while allowing for religion as one among the important components of society. The nation was inclusive of all citizens and their undeniable rights of equal status, as stated in the Constitution. It was rooted in a society that was plural in character and endorsed multiculturalism. Hence the need to at least accommodate, if not integrate, diverse cultures.

Nationalism in India in these times frequently carries the qualifier of Hindu nationalism or religious nationalism, which makes it more explicitly religious in nature and emphasizes the status of the dominant majority. But such nationalism is no longer a national movement that includes every citizen as being of equal status with equal rights, as was aspired to in the earlier understanding of nationalism.

If our cultural identity is going to be moulded, unavoidably, by some inheritance from the past, and which we preserve and comprehend in the history we accept—if we are claiming historical heritage as essential—then the history it draws upon has to be accurate. Can we ensure that history, as taught, or read, or projected in the media, is reliable and accurate?

THIS IS WHERE EDUCATION BECOMES CRUCIAL. To use the historical method requires training. It requires trained and competent teachers who can encourage students to ask questions about what they are learning, and can handle their enquiries with some knowledge. Both are given little attention in current educational training. The questions should not be casual comments but thoughtful and critical inquiries. This would lead to a better understanding of who we are and why we live the way we do. Such questions pose problems not as obstructions, but to encourage further exploration in the search for answers.

History as an awareness of heritage begins in school. When we think of schools today, we tend to think of state schools. We often forget that much of the schooling is in the hands of religious or quasi-religious institutions—gurukuls, shishu mandirs, madrasas and convents. In a democratic society, educational institutions should ideally be delinked from religion. This would allow a greater emphasis on doubting, questioning, considering alternate explanations and working out explanations based on logical and rational thinking—all of which is the primary function of education. In state schools at least, this should be the foundation of the educational programme. Imagination and fantasy have a place in the appreciation of creative literature and the arts, but less so in the social sciences. What we may, on rare occasions, think of as an imagined possibility about the past can at most provide a theme to be researched, but the research itself cannot be based on imagination.

There was a time when students in state schools were given an education that had some degree of quality in terms of a basic understanding of the world in which they lived. This is woefully scarce today. It is not thought necessary that students should be taught to comprehend and question, if they wish to, the society which is their ambience. There is little or no recognition of the fact that questioning it is a way of understanding it and, ultimately, necessary to improving it. The purpose of education today has become one in which students are required to memorize information from their textbooks—whether relevant or not—often in question-answer form, rather than being encouraged to think critically and enquire about the world they live in. Education is fast becoming a form of catechism, and this denies the faculty of thinking independently.

The textbooks currently prescribed merely provide information, and not always the most reliable. That is why in 2006, a few of us professional historians demanded that, at least in state schools, textbooks in all subjects be written, or at least supervised, by professionals in the subject. But this demand was ignored by the authority that controlled education. Today, the treatment of the subject by those in authority is so casual that it has been announced that sections of history—for example, the Mughal period—will be deleted from the textbooks. This is referred to as the 'rationalization' of the syllabus—a term used by the NCERT (National Council of Educational Research and Training). By 'rationalization' they mean that the Mughal period, or any other they choose, need not be taught. The cover-up for such actions is the claim that it makes the curriculum lighter and easier for the student.

But deleting huge and important segments of history is not the answer, since that makes the subject opaque and difficult to follow. What answer will be given when the student asks, 'Who were the Marathas fighting, and why?' 'Did nothing important happen in the two centuries from the sixteenth to the eighteenth—the centuries that have been omitted?' 'Who built the Taj Mahal?'

At the university level, if portions of the syllabus are deleted, as has been threatened, and reading lists pruned without explanation, it will result in reducing or eliminating the intellectual challenge of the subject. Not only is this new history questionable, but it does not reflect the debates that are often the focus in professional history. Reading lists are pared down and the writings of historians who are disapproved of are removed. Lectures by visiting scholars—Indian or foreign—are disallowed unless permission is obtained from those controlling the university.

Some of us who were involved in the establishing of the Jawaharlal Nehru University in the early 1970s have been appalled by the backsliding transition that it has undergone in the last ten years. Other universities and some strong centres of the social sciences, in particular, have also suffered. The social sciences are especially vulnerable since political ideologies are anxious to control them when they plan to introduce changes in social institutions, and such changes are questioned by social scientists. In establishing the JNU, we were determined to show that Indian academics were capable of establishing a university that would be highly respected, both at home and in the world. In this we succeeded. But now in the last decade maintaining academic standards has been made extremely problematic—to put it very politely.

As has been pointed out by many academics, this control has been imposed in various ways: through appointing a few substandard members of faculty in each of the centres; by non-professionals dictating curricula and syllabi; by attempts to rescind the appointments of existing professors emeritus and discouraging students from reading their writings; by curtailing the freedom to research and teach what academics regard as meaningful themes that advance the discipline; by disallowing invitations to foreign specialists in a subject should they be persons disapproved of by the government; and by generally exercising interference and control over the work and activities of the institution, to the point of negating the freedom of professionals to maintain the quality required of such institutions.

In 2020, the situation went beyond academic mechanisms of control. A large, vicious mob armed with lathis was allowed into the JNU campus at night, shouting 'Jai Shri Ram' and physically attacking students and faculty, breaking the furniture and creating terror all round. An attack on Jamia Millia Islamia led to the vandalization of a part of its library, which was justified by the claim that the police were searching for 'urban Naxals'.

On other occasions there have been arrests of students for criticizing authority. Some of those arrested have now remained in jail for six years, without trial. Intellectually purposeful education requires an ambience where there is freedom to think and to question. Political controls on education silence intellectual creativity.

Arresting those in political opposition and those holding political positions in diverse political parties is an old colonial habit that continued into independent India. But in the last decade there appears to have been a wider spread of the net, with additional professions being drawn in. Without doing a head count, one has the impression that apart from those professionally in political opposition, there are now a large number of people caught in the net who are not professional politicians. The sixteen arrested in the Bhima Koregaon case were academics, social scientists, lawyers, social workers, writers and poets. They were and are people working for social causes, but they are not remotely the terrorists or assassins whose actions would justify arrest. These are glimpses of the prevalent anti-intellectualism.

THIS EXPLAINS—up to a point—why the social sciences are marginalized in the educational curriculum, since they are concerned with analysing the functions of society and inevitably involve assessing the effectiveness of the projects that govern us. History, in particular, is vulnerable because the justification for acts of governing relates to the ideology that provides the supposed impetus, and this in turn draws a large part of its legitimacy from history.

The history researched and written by professional historians is being replaced by interpretations that historians no longer hold. This supposedly new history emphasizes the superiority of the Aryans, and insists on a glorious Hindu period in which Hindu civilization was ahead of all others in the world, but which was severely damaged in the succeeding period of Muslim rule, in which the history of India consisted mainly of the damage done to Hindu society by the Muslims. It explains the history of medieval India on the basis of the two-nation theory. It claims to replace what others have been writing and teaching in the last seventy-five years, in post-colonial times. Much of this previous history is now labelled as Marxist, even if it is not. With this label, it is said to be erroneous, is abused, and dismissed.

LET ME DIGRESS SLIGHTLY to discuss what is required in a Marxist analysis of history, which has a distinctive historical theory of explanation. Those who rush to accuse professional historians of being Marxists appear not to be familiar with Marxist approaches to history. The latter touch on many aspects and have been widely debated, as a result of which some arguments have been accepted but others rejected—a process common to the application of many theories of explanation, irrespective of whether they are explicitly non-Marxist or are of any sub-brand of Marxism.

Many theories of explanation have been put forward, some in detail, others more broadly. They have been widely discussed—for instance, the theories of Positivism, or of Max Weber, Michel Foucault, Antonio Gramsci, and others. Nor is this a matter of considering only European philosophers, because we have to recognize that so far there have not been any Indian thinkers of historically viable but different explanations of how Indian history has evolved and why changes occurred in history and the forms those changes assumed. Even the European philosophers involved in the search for such explanations are modern thinkers, since the search for explanations—rather than just narrating what happened—is a modern idea. It evolved in European philosophy and then caught the intellectual concerns of others. Ancient societies, whether Indian or Greek or Chinese, focused on narrating what it was thought had happened in the past. Their narrations were represented both by repeating the earlier version or altering it to suit the requirements of their own times. Accuracy about what happened in the past was not given the same primacy as its representation. But what each group believed to be the essential representation of the past differed from one to the other.

The fact that historical writing has moved from narratives to explanations of what is narrated leads to tracking the links between ideas and activities, especially as located in the social arena. Various nineteenth-century theories attempted to do this, and among those that received considerable attention in the late nineteenth and early twentieth centuries were the explanations proposed by Karl Marx and by Max Weber. Marx's historiography became a much-discussed theory of explanation. It was used creatively by some to further the dimension of analysis and dismissed by others who denied its usefulness.

Marxist historiography is not restricted to what is often its incorrect description, that of economic determinism. Economic factors are important, but not the key to every explanation. Marxist analysis has a broader assessment of what went into the making of a historical event, which evokes a wide social spectrum. His theories drew on ideas that were being widely discussed by philosophers and scientists in the nineteenth century.

One among these was the investigation of whether the socio-economic context has a bearing on the form and employment of ideas. This has been helpful, for example, in analysing the link between religion—both ritual and belief—and the influence on society of institutions connected with it. This marks a move away from explaining everything as being fundamentally related to religion.

Associated with this has been an interesting discussion on the impact of what might have been contradictory ideas or even opposing forces in society. The notions of dissent of the Shramana religions that questioned the ideas propagated by Brahmanism form an interesting example that is only now beginning to be investigated. Dissenting opinion sometimes reveals aspects of society that had not been either thought of or pursued with sufficient rigour. This also ties into the presence of dialectical thinking that goes back to the philosophical debates of earlier times, as I have mentioned.

Widely discussed theories have focused on the evolution of institutions involved in shaping various social forms. A frequent question has been whether human society evolved from the simpler forms of hunter–gatherer groups and pastoral societies to the more complicated forms of large village settlements and eventually to urban centres. Contributions from ideas of evolution and some anthropological studies of early societies strengthened these ideas. Why did certain societies evolve and change, whereas others remained as they were for substantial periods?

This inevitably raised many questions, such as that of ranking societies in a hierarchy—which was a major concern of the last century—and ascertaining why a society used a particular theory to justify its ranking of social groups. Explanations of caste ranking in India since early historical times have been discussed and are still being debated. There are as yet no definitive answers; nevertheless, the recognition that the structure of caste did change over time, and the attempts to investigate what changed, mark a departure from treating it as a static form of social organization. Questions such as these often determined the contours of social forms. Some theorists saw them as independent forms; others saw them as an evolutionary pattern.

It is important to remember that the application of Marxism to history is not primarily for formulating a political organization, but for using a theory to explain how a society functioned in past times and what its consequences are in the present day. To reduce it to a political issue and associate it only with terrorist groups that claim to be Maoists is to show a lack of understanding of its intellectual questioning of historical explanations and philosophical explorations.

All such theories of explanation can either provide a convincing explanation or a partial one or can be viewed as inadequate or incorrect and set aside. We don't have to be frightened of such theories or run away from them, or abuse those who hold them. Instead, one can show where they may be viable and where they are not. Some Marxist analyses have been discarded: an obvious example is a flawed theory—that of the Asiatic mode of production—which historians found untenable, deriving as it does from the colonial understanding of Asian society as envisaged in the concept of Oriental Despotism.

The more clearly defined social formations such as those essential to historical materialism—slavery, feudalism, capitalism—were based on the history of Europe, and have been tested to see if any, or all as a pattern, were applicable to the Indian past. The debate on feudalism among Indian historians, for example, resulted in a historically worthwhile series of studies of medieval Indian history. In both contesting the mode or trying to apply it, new facets of the sources were revealed, and other aspects that provided a much fuller picture of that period, especially with reference to regional history.

All theories pertaining to current knowledge in any discipline are open to change when new information is discovered or fresh ways of analysing data are worked out. This requires that we recognize that historiography—the study of the writing of history—also undergoes change. Analyses made at one point in time may have to change if new sources and explanations become available and the context changes. Historians are not disconnected from change, but nevertheless they have to adhere to using only proven evidence. Explanations have to be updated, or perhaps even reconsidered, if there is strikingly new reliable evidence that questions the existing interpretations.

An important aspect of theories of explanation is the concept of change. How and why do societies undergo change? Is it intrinsic to social functioning, or does it require an external agency? The idea of evolution became central to the notion of change, and much discussion focused on what actually causes it. Here the idea of the dialectic seemed helpful in the search for an answer. Since knowledge is based on explanation, an initial dialectical analysis examining different points of view can be useful. As applied to society, it assumes that an existing situation could be opposed by an alternate one, and that through the contradiction between the two, something new would emerge.

This method was used in Indian philosophical debates since early times in the concept of *purvapaksha-pratipaksha-siddhanta* / the proponent, the opponent and the emerging message, where the opposition of one to the other could lead to the emergence of a new form. It is present in the Socratic method in the mid–first millennium BCE in Greece, as also in recent times in Hegel and others. The philosophers of ancient times who employed versions of the dialectical method were, of course, not Marxists. Explanations do change, sometimes, because the discovery of fresh sources is itself unpredictable; but a viable explanation requires proven evidence and logical, rational argument.

IT HAS NOW ALSO BECOME FASHIONABLE to accuse academic historians of writing history in a style too dense to be easily comprehended. Often they are then accused of being Marxists! The accusation is used to justify a pop version of history, believed to be more accessible to the general public, even if such a version contradicts that of professional historians. It is claimed that people prefer to read whatever the pop writers put out as history, since it is easily comprehended.

It is surprising that intelligent people can support such a meaningless explanation. Do they not pause to think that if the finer points and nuances of a discipline have become a little more technical over the past century, then those wishing to learn from reading it have to prepare themselves by acquiring a basic familiarity with the primary forms of the changes currently associated with the discipline? Such preparation would normally be given by improving the quality of school and university education to incorporate the new changes. Had the quality of education not deteriorated so rapidly in recent years, academic history writing would have been accessible, as it had been earlier at a time when education was at a higher level of learning.

The fault is not that of academic historians but rather of those whose literacy has not kept pace with what is required. One may also ask why, of all the social sciences, it is only in history that there is such heavy opposition from those using the media. Given the advances in knowledge, keeping up with a subject does require reading on the subject and at least understanding how it is being analysed, even if not doing the analysis oneself.

There were no such complaints about the density of writings in economics after the induction of mathematics into economics: those interested in the arguments about the economics of a problem simply took it upon themselves to understand the mathematics involved. Academic economists did not bother to make themselves understood to the general public, nor were their more up-to-date writings dismissed as Marxist. It is recognized that the study of economics may also have some politics in its theories of explanation, but this is far less contested. A possible reason for this is that whereas the claim to a historical reading can provide legitimacy for political action, this does not apply to the same extent in disciplines other than history.

The situation differs, therefore, where a discipline has a more evident political role involving more extensive publicity. In order to be widely and immediately accepted by the general public, the proponents of their kind of history are active on the varied media. This brings instant publicity and huge audiences. It publicizes what anyone wishes to write, whether it be sensible or nonsensical, since there is no one to assess it.

Everyone is free to present what they want to. One cannot object to that. It is part of the freedom of expression to which every citizen has a right. However, when it is claimed that what is being presented is historically accurate, but in fact it is not, then the professional historian can legitimately object. More often, though, the professional historian chooses to disregard such claims and carries on quietly with his or her research.

The work and views of professional historians are often misquoted, or quoted out of context, sometimes even distorted, and often simply not understood. This becomes one excuse for targeting and trolling them.

Correcting such claims is absurdly time-consuming and, in any case, no amount of correction will put an end to them. Their purpose is not to establish historical accuracy but to censor those who challenge history-on-the-media or even the history that has official approval. But surely the personal abuse of the professional historian is not called for. This reflects the lack of civility in our society.

ALL THIS SUGGESTS that there is one more function of fake history that should be self-evident. This is its political function. In some situations, it is the primary function; therefore, it is up front and propagated with great vehemence. Occasionally, this is done in a more subtle manner. Given the centrality of history to the construction of national and cultural identity, history becomes problematic if it draws from hearsay or supports an obviously dubious agenda. If a particular history has an agenda, this will become apparent in the ideology that it propagates, which determines its intention. Its reading of the past is directed in such a way as to try to legitimize the making of society according to that agenda.

We have to remind ourselves that historically we do have a strong tradition of questioning ideas, beliefs and practices, but to which we have not given enough attention in our studies of the past. We had strong dissenting sects such as those of the Shramanas who opposed Brahmanism. Jainism, included among the Shramana religions, flourished in some regions of the subcontinent such as Karnataka and Gujarat and was less clearly present in other areas. Buddhism slowly moved out of India—or, as some have argued, was exiled from India—and was established in other parts of Asia as the dominant religion and, even in exile, was more widespread and significant than Brahmanism or what came to be called Hinduism, which remained largely concentrated in the subcontinent. What has not yet been investigated is whether Buddhism was deliberately exiled or whether it slowly faded away for a variety of reasons, and what these reasons were. Or indeed, whether some of what it taught was inducted into the emergence of new religious sects that arose in the late first and early second millennium CE. An exploration of these questions is needed.

Viewed historically, religious nationalism, or Hindutva as some call it, is a new turn in the politics of India. It is not identical with Hinduism but is a new formulation that tries to appropriate both Hinduism as a religion and the history of India as a source of its legitimacy from the past. Both have had to be reformulated to suit the purposes of Hindutva. It is not just the recognition of a continuing form of dissent from the older accepted historical interpretations of the past, which had not been emphasized by historians earlier—such as in the teachings of the nastikas / non-believers—but the deliberate reformulation of the past as a form of history that provides legitimacy for a particular current political ideology. This is a new feature of post-colonial times, although it carries the imprint of colonial interpretations, and it dates to the past century. This is where examining the political use of Hindutva becomes necessary. The political ideology seeking legitimation from history and embedded in a particular interpretation of history is what we have to recognize. Its recognition becomes visible in its claim to being historical, even if this is a questionable claim.

This is what I have been discussing here and suggesting—that as a form it is new to the history of our society, both intellectually and in practice. Such political and social changes are only too familiar from other histories as they have evolved in the past century in different parts of the world. In some societies fake history has had a traumatic political fallout. These latter have been the inspiration for some of the most devastating annulling of ethics and values. Earlier, one was jubilant at its having been banished from the societies where it had occurred. But its recurrence in various forms—big or small—is a fearful prospect. It would be useful to know how history can be used in various political ways.

The historical legitimation of this political ideology took shape as similar to but not identical with movements in various societies, and in some more recently than in others. One characteristic has been that they were anti-democratic and opposed to the freedom of speech and the right to dissent. Nor did all citizens in these societies have equal rights. The distribution of inequality varied according to genetic origins, social history and occupations. The pattern of the economies varied, as did the role of religion in these diverse societies. The denial of freedom of expression accompanies fake history, as this is claimed as the authentic history and cannot be questioned.

In listing some of these historical movements that were essentially anti-democratic and often also anti-secular, one thinks of diverse societies. Bolshevism in Russia lasted longer than most others, starting with the Bolshevik Revolution in 1917 and declining in the mid-1950s. It had both similarities and dissimilarities with later movements; its focus, however, was less on the past and more on the present. The 1930s and '40s saw the rise and fall of Nazism in Germany and the Fascisti in Italy, both cut short by World War II. Racism was a key feature of their ideology. They were followed soon after, in the 1950s but less effectively, by McCarthyism in the United States, which focused on censoring people accused of supporting Marxism and Leftist ideologies. As is common to many such movements, that which is being disapproved of—such as the disallowing of free thought—is precisely what is practised at that time by those in authority. Redefining the past blazed forth in Mao Zedong's dramatic Great Proletarian Cultural Revolution in China. Similar movements, although perhaps a trifle less intensive, are later associated with other countries and are not unknown to this day.

Barring the Bolshevik Revolution, which lasted longer, the rest were effective for a decade or a little more, but the after-effects lasted much longer. The usual rights of free citizens were disallowed except for the dominant majority community; the racial superiority of the community that constituted the majority was insisted upon; and the enemy within was the minority identified by race and religion and systematically annihilated—or at least sought to be extinguished. In each case, the devastation of the societies where they had a presence was immense.

The parallel is so close to what is happening in some countries in our time that the future becomes rather frightening. The ready-to-hand diagnosis for the twenty-first century continues to be the tendency to dub every activity that is disapproved of as the work of terrorists. This is not to deny that there are active terrorists, but there are multiple reasons for such activities, and it would be wise to be aware of these rather than attribute everything to a single cause. Interestingly, it is also noticeable that the ethic of tolerance and non-violence has ceased to be mentioned in our discourses, whether private or public.

The historical question that needs asking is whether these ideologies, and the actions based on them, could have been avoided. Is this pattern of change inevitable when a radically different ideology is imposed on a society transitioning from former feudal or colonial systems into a nation-state? Such an argument would not apply, perhaps, in every one of the above-mentioned cases, but explanations for the mutation must be sought. Comparative studies are unavoidable.

In a sense, what we are faced with is a post-nationalist condition, when nation-states have been established but there is uncertainty about the form they will take.

Another question that is now being asked is whether political dictatorship and the system it requires can be described as a facet of the battle between nationalism and modernity. Nationalism, when it is qualified by race or religion or language and then taken to an extreme, can turn into fascism and become the opposite of modernity, in that it denies democracy and individual freedom. The potential of such a condition emerging as a mark of post-nationalism can be a threat.

We need to ask ourselves whether we in India have overcome these attempts and confrontations, or whether we have to be vigilant at the possibility of such events. And, if this is where we are, we need to ensure that they remain something in passing, as they have been so far when it comes to the larger continuity of history. An intelligent reading of the history of the last century should give us this awareness so that we can recognize the signs. False alarms there might be, but these can be set aside by analysing what we may recognize as symptoms.

Awareness involves understanding why this ideology is seemingly attractive and assessing how it has injured each of the societies that I have mentioned. The task of comprehending what a society requires, and the absence of which encourages the violent solutions that the ideology supports, should not be brushed aside. This ideology in its various manifestations is what gives, to those who endorse it, the power to destroy the best in a society. This is perhaps better understood through an awareness of the political message implicit in the changes currently being insisted upon in the rewriting of what until now has been the accepted history of India—rewriting that does not conform to the history as written by professional historians. This, in part, is what I have been concerned with in what I have said so far.

WE COME TO THE QUESTION with which I started and with which I shall end: has the future been forsaken in all this? For those of us who, as nations, entered the modern age after overthrowing colonialism, what follows requires a clear direction. The question in our times is: will we be able to retrieve the vision we had as part of anti-colonial nationalism—of making India an independent, democratic, secular nation? In 1947, we envisioned becoming a society with a heritage of freedom of thought that had enabled us to debate consent and dissent. We were exploring the ways of establishing the rights of citizens. We rightly prided ourselves when we succeeded in establishing crucial rights, as, for instance, adult franchise. This is why what appears to be the scuttling of this right, with changes in electoral procedures, is regarded with suspicion and apprehension today.

So strong was our past commitment to a free society that we were able, through an election, to defeat a significant attempt to silence us by using the powers of the Emergency. This achievement was rooted in a historical heritage of both consent and dissent and a commitment to humanism. But today we are enmeshed in a different reading of what is being projected as our cultural heritage, and we need to recognize its ramifications, as well as its uses by those who author it; how education and the new agencies of propagation, such as social and other media, are being subordinated to it; and to its political use. Not to mention the wilful erasing of some of our more significant history in the process.

Let us also keep in mind that history is a continuous process, and together with the changes that are made in our patterns of living come problems that some of these changes introduce. The universe that is imminent in the future is one that neither we nor those who govern us comprehend. Our world is now open to the unknown impact of the unpredictable. The first uncertainty is how climate change will alter our environment and therefore our ways of living and thinking and the pattern of our culture. The second uncertainty is how artificial intelligence will force us to restructure our lives in unthought-of ways. At this moment we do not know whether we can turn these unpredictable happenings to our advantage, or whether we will have to succumb to them.

Let me, in conclusion, leave you with a couple of questions.

Will we still be able to nurture a society whose parameters are open to debate and discussion? A society is constituted of all kinds of people who, whatever culture they endorse, should have equal status as citizens. Or are we willing to confine our society to a single, limited, uniform way of living and thinking? Will there be only one explanation of the past, with all others subsumed in the one or else dismissed? Is culture going to be defined by the cultural idiom of the dominant majority? Will variants be disallowed, as has happened already in some cultural spheres?

A university or a research institute is the apex of the education system. These are unique institutions entitled to freedom of expression, with teachers and students able to discuss their ideas without fear of being silenced. They have the potential to be the cradle of creativity. In a university, this freedom is not a luxury but a necessity. It is a precondition to the advancement of knowledge. Knowledge can advance only when existing knowledge is questioned and more incisive explanations are sought. This is demonstrated with clarity wherever there have been advances in various disciplines, as in the sciences. Why are we so ready to subvert it?

Do we have to keep struggling against pretend history and the damage it is doing—not only to what we know to be our history, but also to our cultural heritage, educational system and political future? How can we return to exploring history as we once did, in a thoughtful and sensitively intelligent way, understanding the past more closely and reliably, observing what links it to the present, and what we might see in it as a viable future? Ultimately, the decision of what we should do is ours.